Petrolhead

Jenny Hope

Oversteps Books

First published in 2010 by

Oversteps Books Ltd
6 Halwell House
South Pool
Nr Kingsbridge
Devon
TQ7 2RX
UK

www.overstepsbooks.com

Oversteps Books acknowledges with thanks the financial
assistance of Arts Council England, South West

Printed in Great Britain by imprint digital, Devon.

For Ian, Lissy and Oscar

Acknowledgements

Acknowledgements are due to the editors of the following publications and websites in which poems or versions of them have previously appeared: Envoi, The Interpreter's House, Iota, JBWB, Obsessed by Pipework, Raw Edge, The Rialto, Six by Nine, www.artscouncil.org, www.daisygoodwin.co.uk, www.ukauthors.com.

Special thanks are due to family and friends for their support, especially Michele Lefevre, Jean Armstrong, Louisa Cannon, John Lawrence, Chris Long, Faith Walsh.

Extra special thanks to John Lawrence for his close reading on many occasions.

Thanks also to David Hart, Roz Goddard, Victoria Field, Rose Flint, Alicia Stubbersfield for their help and inspiration.

Finally I would like to thank my editor, Alwyn Marriage, for all her hard work, input and patience.

And always Ian, Lissy and Oscar.

Artwork on front cover: *Fire* © Mark Pettifer

Contents

Blue

My first addiction
clear as sky and stretched-out
Saturday afternoons,

our long dawdles to the filling-station kiosk
for the pocket-money power
of everlasting sweets.

That tight-edged scent
sharp as light inside me.
It cut my lungs to blood.

Later we'd slip past
hip-handled pumps
for the forbidden naked flame

and secreted packets of ten.
A few minutes up the lane
and through the lush grass

and meadow flowers.
We could be lovers, yes?
your accent harsh against my skin.

No! I drew myself together.
You shrugged off displeasure
like a stolen scarf.

Tarmac

I

At last a proper stretch of road.
You can tell its quality, the smooth noise
under tyres and hushed-up spray.
See how it slicks down the valley
like well-oiled tagliatelle?

You loved the smell of new-laid roads.
You'd smell their scent from miles away and perch
on hot-metalled fences and suck in the scented heat
of bitumen and dust. The road was stripped down to basics;
you'd strip off your top to mimic the greased-up workmen,
your shoulder scrubbed as smooth as an egg.
They laughed and asked if you could give them a hand.

You gave them more than that; chickens in fact.
You were just too slow.
Years later, your brother asked me out.

II

To lay a road correctly you have to be prepared
to strip back your soul to the bare essentials.
It's no good holding back, that outer skin has to go.

Then you're there, admiring the scored sub-surface,
looking for the uneven texture that needs fixing.

III

Have you ever watched a dog eat a toffee?
It's an unkind fascination. It's that kind of word,
the very sound sticks to your teeth.

I knew a woman once; her husband drove her for miles,
craving for the scent of hot new roads.
It's at its best still sticky-warm,
when it clings to everything it connects with
and fills your mouth with the taint of metal,
that remnant of foil.

Electricity

The sub-station is in a mind all her own,
no doubt dreaming of past days: waters splitting
open over earth, those ancestors lined up
in turbine halls.

She's poked down a half-forgotten street
where she relives that constant movement
of generations. The trees are trying to smother
her, ashamed of their close association.

Stand still for long enough and I swear
you'll see her rocking to her own vibration.

Cheque or Cash?

It's a straight enough question, but you watch him weight
his answer; a hangman deliberating the correct poundage
for the drop of the noose. He looks unsure, can he hear the smug purr
of detachment? Or perhaps he's already picturing the rectangular
sharpness of its one-trick purpose? You could track its progress
though the few bad ones spoil it for the rest.

Cash would speak if you'd let it. It's that bloke down the pub,
that seen-it-done-it chameleon; lairy-loud and twice as fractious,
boasting itself up one moment, then nose-tapping the next.
Cash knows where the action is, and how to avoid it.
It changes appearance to suit its purpose. From crisp and clean,
unhindered by past baggage to well-used notes, softened by fingertip oil
and palm-soft. You could rest your head and sleep a thousand
dreams. You lick your fingers for the merest film of cocaine.

My Father is listening...

in silence with
fingertips
to palms.

Late night frequencies
slip through his
fingers
and rest.

Outside
the world is pinpricked
with streams of tungsten
orange. Toad spawn laid
through liquid skies,
separated by
clear vision.

A rift of Wishbone
Ash escapes from
behind his eyes
as his reflection
gazes
in.

I watch my Mother climbing up walls

Inside her house, she's as deft as a mime.
Her hands palm the vinyl silk but she's stopped
by the ceiling, she's not yet mastered the fly-side-grip.

Instead she sips her tea and considers the complexities
of architecture. She catches the next clear day
and escapes outside. She nooses the neck of the house

and knots its innards around her gut.
Her toes slip into grooves of mortar. She pauses,
restarts; considers each man-made trough

and negotiates her way. Her fingers take each slightest chance
and hold their moment before committing to the next
move up. It's as delicate as climbing ice.

Under the eaves she converses with bats.
Forty-five degrees later she pulls herself upright
and straddles the apex, singing.

Lissy Silverfish

Morning

At 2 a.m. you tighten your grip.
The hospital say come in for eight.
We bathe together – inhale Clary Sage;
buoyant whilst your father dozes.

Before first light I'm wired up to a tens machine.
By dawn I'm counting magpies -
three for a girl.

Afternoon

The window overlooks the loading bay.
Two men manoeuvre a corpse –
its bin-bagged body obvious.
Your father says – *don't look.*

Evening

You arrive silent, knowing, into electric twilight.
You rise to greet me, vernix-silver gleams like hope.
Your father cuts the cord that binds us –
makes you whole.

Night

We're separated by clear vision.
Nurses have wrapped you against the world.
I feed you. You put flesh to your name.

Sir Oscalot

At 2 a.m. things got too quick –
your dad faffed about
putting everything in the car
we would never need.

Five minutes from home
you began to push
with too many cars on the road
heading in the other direction.

The hospital arrived a moment too soon.
I slapped on to the car park. Smokers
thought we'd rowed and waited
for the next instalment.

I want to push, smokers stubbed out,
came running, chaired me in.
Moments later the midwife's words:
a little boy, is that who you were expecting?

Re: Visit

The school has shrunk to fill these bones. Parquet
floors on which a hundred infant bodies swam
or skated in grey-bottomed socks reflect
the years. Small corridors house waist-high names.
Bright walls hide behind clumsy alphabets.
The teacher's desk is wood well-worn smooth
and perches high above with headed gaze.
The moment holds a photograph's pose. With
just one push I could slip across the room.
I find myself locked in as particles
of eager sun slip inside and sparkle
beneath the dust. Parents stoop to enter
and collect the end of the afternoon
those tired heads too young to still remember.

Last Day at School

Your final day arrives to this; steaming July,
a swarm of girls ready to sting.

The teachers can't be bothered to enforce the rules,
not for these last few hours. *They'll have a rude awakening.*

Girls open pencil cases, locate Biros with chewed-off ends;
the result from endless double biology.

You're next.

Slapper, fag-face, grot-bag; keep in touch;
hair drawn under arms, twelve o'clock shadow;
old fart, slag! Love and kisses.

You're marked for the rest of the day.

You wander home past shorn verges
and butchered hedgerows; fledglings gone.

You take your time between then and now.
Your shirt is a tattoo of signatures and questionable words.

Your father takes one look and asks –
but will it all wash out?

Na Berganta

Under the almond tree my mother squats,
flushes her roots with water.

She reaches east and arches up
to crown the tree;

discards the husk from her own sweet nut.

Tofal's Wood

Estrella nods like a pump-jack.
We follow her trail of crescents.

We're in a wood, one kilometre from Arta.
A stone-stacked wall divides a neighbour's land from us

but we can leap it.
Nearby a finca unwinds, these two weeks it's ours.

Trees hum too low for us to hear;
our footmarks are too heavy.

Ripe *coneja* flash like pimento.
We gather wild rosemary; it's sweeter than back home.

Rocks bead the ground like skulls.
Below Pine and Green Oak,

we smell the warm scent of undergrowth.
They wait for us to go; strip their leaves

Mallorcean Garden

Down by the gate a Honey Buzzard claws at wasps.
Hoops of citrus, mean and black, snap at his head.
Over in the generator house my father weighs his mortality
along with an emergency repair. A rat has bitten through
the pipes. Surely they've got enough cats here?
The house is silent.

He holds it in his fist, it is heart-sized.
He squeezes its strength and examines it from every angle.
The air is dry. The sun burns at the door.
The shelves are full with jars of spare nails
and a chemistry of insecticides. He hears wings.

Down by the gate a Honey Buzzard claws at wasps.
The grab of his foot; squeezes, retracts, squeezes, retracts.
My father watches, angles his head, his eye beads a temple,
his skull ovals, flight fingers splay out and his skinny shoulders beat time.

Venga la Fiesta!

The blood-hot heat crowds around us,
sucks on our skin. Our calves ache with steps

and homage to the long-dry bones of saints.
The market ends. We eat *menu del dia* then lose

our way in tight kept streets. Kiosks set
up for the night, their hot-fatted owners impatient

as we burn our fingers on fresh-cooked churros.
We swap words, our tempers clenched.

Until evening, when heat pads out the town,
pushes itself against my waist. My spine turns

to wax. Mau softens our hard dry mouths.
We find a cool stone alcove. Make love

to the beat of parading drums. Hold tight
that second of stillness as fireworks ignite.

Bone Love

The good folk at A & E had never
seen the like; the ambulance personnel
snorted laughter, dropped the hump-shaped stretcher
and held their sides. *What have we got here then?*

The itch-infested blanket when thrown
back with the magnitude of a serving
waiter revealed two lovers linked together.
The diagnosis was a long-time-dead

(this, due to the obvious lack of skin
and protruding bones.) But despite their life-
worn appearances this couple were still
able to satisfy themselves. In time

they came to prefer the absence of skin
which only hindered the act itself.
Yet it's the mechanics that fascinate
so they mirror-lined their bedroom to view

all angles: *the lotus; crushing spices;
splitting of a bamboo; flower in bloom;
the clinging creeper; the encircling;*
but shut their ears to the clatter of bones.

The Man Who Married His Car

He's underneath her most weekends,
his girl that is; an Austin Allegro,
nineteen-seventy-four on an N-plate.

He calls her Sweetheart; thinks she's fit
and keeps her behind garage doors
tight as his closed-lipped kiss.

It's not her fault her complexion's sallow;
he doesn't take her out much, preferring
the used-up scent of weekday public transport.

He saves her for Sundays and his annual holiday
then spends his fortnight cruising the local streets,
dressed in Sunday beige. They make a convincing couple.

He left her once, briefly, for a Vauxhall Viva, a metallic-bronze
beauty-queen; his head turned by well-honed angles
and a double strip of jewelled lights across her rear.

But there's little comfort in corners, and he soon returned to curves.
Before they take the air, he buffs and smooths his palm
over her child-birthing rump. Her floor pan is exquisite.

He's got the knack of making her purr. She's kitten-smooth,
no doubt due to years of effort and thumbed-up Haynes manuals.
His eyes reflect on hours of polished chrome.

Mrs Medusa's Mayhem

He shuts his eyes during sex. So do I.
Why should he have all the fun?

He liked a conversation, once; valued the muscle of a good brain,
but had trouble keeping pace

and was always careful not to look me in the eye;
sharp as lakes and as yellow. He knew the rules.

But one day the Red-Tops outed me as
"The Woman Who Could Turn a Man to Stone",

too many *"Don't Think Much of Yours"*, and he can't go
beyond skin-deep;
to my body of bone and heart.

With killer comments on killer eels and driving Dodge Vipers;
making my snakes stand on end.

We have three girls; with my eyes and his sparse temper.
He's given to hissy-fits, says our kids slink wild, leave their
cast off skin in the bath.

He doesn't like their slither-hipped swagger in tight-arsed jeans
and says they follow me. Perhaps as well, he couldn't pick a
pot to hiss in.

He thinks he's clever, makes a joke, about how he's the only
married bloke
without a single mirror in the house.

But at night when I'm unshedding, I catch him sneaking a look;
perhaps I should tell him it's rude to stare.

Beef

Mid-morning and she wants the joint slammed
in a screaming-hot oven. She's banging
on about things being done well and good
or not at all. She's as rigid as wood.

Her world's a vision in monochrome,
high-waisted knickers and her monotone
voice drains your skin of every drop of any-
thing that's charitable, good and holy.

But you, you like things undone; room to manoeuvre,
that flex of flesh as it flips when passed over
your lips. It's how you like things – unchecked
not this over-cooked death. You hedge your bets.

You need that howl of blood, a damn good vet
could get you up and running. Respect
is how you phrase it, as at the very least
you want to taste the nature of the beast.

Jalfrezi

Having just turned forty, she's had enough;
her husband's taken her out to celebrate – just the two of them.
She's sucked into black skins, sleek as expectant seals
and underneath she can feel where the bathwater's heat
has cut her skin.

She's ordered Jalfrezi: chicken, extra-hot and spice-laden.
Later her husband will seduce her, peel off her skins
then rest his head.

But now she eats a seekh kebab and savours the tight-spiced lamb
disintegrating on her tongue. Meanwhile a chicken waits in the noise
from the manic kitchen. Unwrapped and counter-bound with legs apart
and a gap where an apple could fit.

Damson Cheese

You wrinkle your nose. My flesh springs back.
Your moon-bloomed damsons squeeze their heads against the pan.
You let them bleed and stain their inner suns.

Don't dilute with water. My mother's out watching.
She's been here; done this. I might as well write – *Hello Mum!*
Do you come this way often: I guess you do?

Two magpies in the next-door field aren't speaking
But instead surf the grass – chest deep. Next time I look
one's gone for sorrow, the other struts the grass.

It's when I sieve out stone and skin and return
to the wide-mouthed pan that you, decide, join me.
Let's kill a god. I wrinkle my nose, your flesh springs back.

High Tea

The small cakes are over-dressed
for the time of day, and sit stacked
on tiers like débutantes in stiff-edged frills,
waiting to fill their cards. They've never done
a day's work in their lives.

A large cake sits elevated and surveys
the table-cloth. She's sandwiched by jam
and buttered-up cream. She doesn't see the point
of fripperies, but regally waits for the cut of the knife
as she needs to prove she's red inside.

Butterflies

To the untrained eye they look like butterflies.
He learnt the art in school, Domestic Science
it's referred to now. Mostly girls, but rarely
a pubescent boy might venture past the threshold
of laughs from his wood-working mates.
His reasoning? He knows the value of a firm wrist
to fold the mixture as light as air. He fills each waiting cup.
He doesn't want to lose a mouthful.

While they're still cooling, he carefully
extracts the upper core. He's still not sure which to add first, jam
or butter-cream? No matter. He slips in a tea-
spoonful of the butter-cream, then some raspberry jam
as clear as a good ruby. He admires its suspension
of seeds. The portion he removed is expertly
dissected, each half laid across a respectable gap.
To the untrained eye they look like butterflies.

Raspberries

Eased from the bush,
each warm hollow
bares a canine.

It's a robust climate;
takes no nonsense,
the coolness stimulates

the buds and a multitude
of fruits; each hood
an intensity of flavour.

Fruit

You fed me. Firm lychees peeled
from goose-bumped flesh of sunset pink.
Figs divide and flower; four quarters; one whole.
Strawberry hearts bleed a head of seeds.

You split a peach. The soft kernel exposed.
On the table, the flushed cheeks of apples.
A pear hangs like a tear from the bowl;
its stem stronger than expected.

First Grey

Outside, bundled against escaping heat;
it's the coldest day so far. I'm your hero
in a soft shell. You sit behind glass;
wrapped up; watch me work
and your face gives nothing away.
My red-cold hands clear rusting leaves.

I whistle, cut the silence. My sound hangs,
heavy as winter washing. You bring tea.
Its heat doesn't touch the sides.
The light follows retreating clocks.
Screwed down by the lid of the sky,
you dream a Snow White death.

Dead Man Sleeping

Still, he hasn't moved. Not in the seconds, hours,
days, since we arrived from the vein of the M6.
That road'll be the death of me, you; us.

We're occupied by window seats while death
warms itself. Together we watch his flesh-white
dough, proven in the oven of his car.

He's chosen a good spot to park up and die.
Our food colds towards us as I share my gaze.
Others notice and you can't help

but hear their self-preserving silence;
questions suppressed like sordid fantasies –
Did he eat here before he died?

He stirs and returns like Lazarus;
leaven bread; sees a string of faces.

A Walk through the Forest

The forest slips its mouth on mine, digs in the scent.
I haven't washed.
No time.

The muscle twitches, and tucked inside the warm green cheek
my footing shifts.

Enzymes drizzle
through a hush of leaves. Light seeps in.

I slough off dead skin.
I'm exposed, my stomach's coat billows to a hill.

Open, expectant. The forest waits for flesh.

Red Coat

I cannot see the house – the forest hides it.
My coat sucks blood; velvet wet.
I am a cut against sharp green.
Gaps through the trees full with abattoir red.

Other walkers will not catch my eye.
Their silence hums.
A thin path leads me home.
I pass my parents; Father's axe is sharp.
Mother stares; her eyes scream *slut!*

The Forest Seamstress

My mother is making my clothes.
I hide behind a screen and trade my shoes for leaf and bark.
I tread more softly.

Brrrch, Brrrch. She feeds her material through blood and branch.
Brrrch. The birds stop to listen. I hear the rustle of skin.
A pool of leaves breathes at her feet.

Mother climbs from bark to twig. She lifts hair from my face,
lets me see. She tells me to climb. She wants the stars. I shake my head.
My mouth is packed with velvet-warm earth.

My mother laughs and rubs my skin with fresh-spun sap. I am her daughter.
She tugs my gut. I climb to please her. My intestines wind through bark and bough.
She rips satin ribbons from remnant skies and lines hidden pools; eye deep
and as watchful. I sense my soul take root.

Some days her belly growls, I run for shelter. She shakes the ground.
The sky fills with swallows' purple light. I hide to find my way back in.
I emerge to fallen leaves. She smells of age and earth. When she dies
I become her. By winter I dress in icy armour. It keeps my heart soft.

The Tree-House Cottage Garden Land

In the tree-house cottage garden land, the world is flat
but on two levels.

I have no skin. My carcass shimmies, one, two, three
(let's make a Waltz). In this split-level world I lack balance
but move between altitudes.

You've planted night-scented stock; shallow breathing,
I listen hard; shift my feet.

I'm standing on your heart.

Woods

I

We find the gate unlatched
The trees breathe with us.
You listen to them, then answer
Yes.

They tug our skin
and let their leaves kiss the skin of another.
They whisper lies
which soon will twist
and darken.

You find the clearing first.
We intrude, unwelcome until we relax,
show our flesh and release our souls.

Their heart explodes.

II

The heat is sealed in
by armfuls of leaves
in generous canopies.

Ferns line the path,
tight fronds reluctant to let go,
for now.

The path shines where feet
have trodden. A well-worn gleam
leads us in to where others wait.

They watch expectantly as we hesitate.
The trees draw closer.
There's no going back.

III

The leaves turn their back on summer and bare their spines.
Our fingers trace the ridges and chart their disintegration
to a flaming glory. We watch their moments of colour,
then they fall, one by one, before they rot and rise.

IV

The trees are brittle.
The sky is bruised by snow.
Silence is heavy.

Underfoot, the earth mourns
while the wood holds its breath
not wanting to intrude.

The sun is respectful
by its absence.
Whilst the cold preserves
the memory.

Wyre Forest

August: already the leaves are pinched by autumn.
The trees are quiet today, visitors unwilling
to risk the rain. The forest looks inward.

A tree clings to a slope; its roots protrude like veins.
As a child, I hid between these feet
and spent the day with my kin, but left before dark-fall.

We leave after lunch. Our children doze in the car like dogs.
And all the while my daughter's voice, like music,
still winds through the trees.

Willow Wood

The mist has brought a layer of rain
as an added distraction. Goose-shit
crowds around your feet. You reflect
on what might have been and wait

for me to speak first. I can't.
My head splits open and a thousand
starlings flare across the sky and towards
the village. For a moment, the sky

looks cluttered; untidy. I stroke the bark.
My fingers find where we carved your initials
and bared the tree's bald flesh. It's discoloured
and the edges have softened over. Yet still

I prise a ridge of bark off with my thumb,
and admire its texture and colour. I kick
off my shoes and chew your bitter skin.
Our world falls silent.

Self-Portrait as a Smooth-Skinned Beech

But do you remember the tree? It overlooks
our childhood home like a lord. Watch me
as I slip my waist between its skin and raise my arms
in celebration of something yet to happen.

My roots twist like fingers into the quarry's side.
I guess my position is built on trust.
I'd have moved me if I had been them, when they
might have noticed this skinny-ringed sapling

and perhaps thought what sort of trouble
a fully grown specimen might have caused.
But they hadn't built the house then.
This land was a half-forgotten quarry.

Their grandparents hadn't been born.
By the time they'd got their act together
I was already well-established. Sometime
in my teens, I lost the will for ears, preferring

the vibrations of my own kind. In my forties
I gave away my eyes, and in my seventies I allowed
the wind my voice having proved my actions
would suffice. I go by scent and touch and believe me

when I claim they serve me more than well
now I'm multi-limbed. I'm quite the crone.
Grey squirrels root through my hair for facets
of beech mast and I wear a pigeon nest up high.

Wind

At night it demands to be let in;
a starving dog, its voice harsh
against your window.

You ignore the whining and the wind turns
tail and storms through the wood
marking scent.

Later it returns contrite from broken trees
and butts against the glass.

You sneak the window open and you're done for,
until morning when day relents and you wake,
exhausted.

My Neighbour's Garden

She hands me bags of fresh-cut salad, all mixed-up leaves,
mizuno and wild rocket shaded green and heavy red;
the colour of old blood.

She adds handfuls of herbs, slender limbs of chives,
parsley and coriander leaves.

She tells me to eat it fresh and neat, or with a splash
of extra virgin oil.

She says the flavour's all its own
daily watering is the key.

She'd invite me over for lunch someday, but
somehow we never make it to the table despite its proximity.

She admires the sunflowers leaning against her wall;
Velvet Queen, a plush-red and with many faces.

U.S.T.

All summer, we worked in a windowless
office, our days dry-throated, words unformed.

Each morning burned right through. It hadn't rained
in weeks. Forecasters promised us a storm;

nothing came. The air conditioning was
broken. Thin cotton stuck to needled skin.

I inhaled, held my breath, the gap within
heavy, impossible to hold. I watched

you, lips parted, your nape cupped by the ghost
of my hand. Whilst overnight the heat

smouldered, draining us; exhausting August.
And, all that summer, you kept a distance,

not ever coming near; except to ask
a question. Your voice pitched low, soft, secret.

Strange Bedfellows

She's at it again, sneaking off.
Says she needs some time alone;
personal space, that sort of crap.
I know precisely what she's doing.

I fix my eyes to the bedroom floor.
My ears strain over subdued
television as I listen, waiting for
the tell-tale sound of turning

on a worn mattress. She lies to keep
it from me, even done it in the bath
before now; as if I'd not find out.
I find the bastards under the bed.

Spread-eagled, with soft-worn creases
down their curving spines. I want
to break them; snap them right
back. But it's not just men.

She likes women too. Her soft fingers
dip between compliant folds. Tight
secrets once bound in saddle stitch
are revealed. The mattress sighs.

She's coming back.

Petrolhead

At first you fear your flesh might scorch
then burn. You stand upwind to watch him
step inside his rope enclosure. He strips half-naked.

He is magnificence personified and before you know
it you're calculating lung capacity, his projected output
and trajectory. You can do the maths.

When he's not looking you steal his cloth;
soak up sweat between your breasts, mop your brow.
He spots your potential; your dog-eyed adoration.

A little less water, he's more volatile; more water
and he's tame; doused out. You might control him if you tried,
but he's incandescent. You could scrape your finger

across his skin, skim off the excess
then suck your finger dry. Have you never tasted petrol?
Felt that sharp cut on the tongue

as it seeps beneath your skin? No?
Instead you watch him stamp and arch his back.
Transfixed. Aroused.

You buy him take-out cake and coffee
and watch him gorge between displays.
He says the job has numbed his sense

of taste. He no longer eats for pleasure,
everything's just fuel. But still you wish it was your tongue
slipping down his throat, as you wonder what he tastes like.

Walk: interrupted

A walk interrupted by a stomach of rain.
Our sky is weathered by the barn. It holds out its pocket
and draws shut behind us. Clouds clench to fists.
The next-door Friesians have slumped to graze.

You undress without speaking. You discard your clothes like secrets.
They puddle your feet; obsolete.

Unhindered, the simplicity of your lines astonishes me.
The heavens break. You ask,
what's stopping you?

Pebble Beach

I pocket hate from a hidden cove I visit often, and alone.
Hard as hearts and greyer than a judgment call,
it fits into my hand like a fist.

My fingers cage the porous skin
but cannot contain its face, and beneath my thumb
a fault echoes my lifeline.

I weight my anger; compact and ready to be thrown.
It solidifies to fill my palm.

An inverted scab rubs and irritates my flesh.
I lick it clean.

Boxing Night

Your cough drives you from the fire.
The soft sound of shoe on startled frost
sets my teeth on edge. You head beneath
the damson tree – *first to flower, last to fruit* –
planted the year I was born.

I watch you from the window. Your clothes reflect the sky.
Your stomach's swollen, damson-firm, yet out of season.
You're wrapped in ghost-light. I leave you be.

Inside my mother shovels drifts of trifle.
Next morning, she comments on your double-headed
footprints, and asks me if the grass might bruise.

Dark Slug

Dark slug;
dirty little thing
weights your shoulder,

knots you in
eating your balance.
You flick it

but it's suctioned.
I try to talk
it from your neck,

it's a race to peel
before it reaches
your inner ear

and squirms in.
Once there it'll
take some shifting.

So far it's still
soft and malleable,
killable with salt.

Riddle

I lick my face from the plate of the moon,
come clean to reflect on the fleece-white 'glow.
I've not time for sleep, much to do. Livestock
ought a hex or two; perhaps a visit.

Sailors curse me; at sea I cause a storm,
while on land if I hold straight, scare-wits
shiver. I speak with stark, ungodly cry,
run long bones ragged, cut through the parish.

Another trick? I make chaste brides turn from church;
let stretched shadows hound me from my form.
For thirst I'll suck your cattle, bone and dry;
but to sup my flesh may snare both sorrow

and despair. Life furrows the old straight track
as I shift, from buck to doe, buck and back.

Ewes' Milk

The earth-light is concentrated
and cuts my skin
like water cuts a thirst.

The day's crust rises,
swells then splits
to display my bones.

The air will feast
on marrowfat, sweet marrowfat
and grow sleek

and comely like a wife.

Market Day

Cold February banks before dawn and litters the ground with snow-eyed splinters.
The stalls are in place. The egg lady has stopped selling;
she tells me she's too old for this, hands tremor as she passes me her final box.

My skin grumbles, I take the change. The air is bitter and tastes of blood.
I was here last month. I come here every month.
They know me now, by face but not by name.

They sell me their honey, cheese and local-brewed beer.
Would they run, I wonder, if I ever paused and spoke out loud?

I scan the sky. The weather turns inside.

Equinox

A cut and paste day,
in a cut and paste life.

I sip American Tan tea.
The sky as coloured

as three pigeons sit
on the half-cut Rowan tree.

So now I'm thinking
how the day comes at you

like a sail.
My mind's a handbag,

faulty strapped,
with toothless zip.

The farmer's left
his meadow half-mowed;

ever shrinking islands
contract, implode

and perhaps that's it –
going, going, gone?

Samhain

We ride the trees, their boughs hold out hands
like eager children, wanting to be touched.

Do you remember when?

That old man's turnpike cottage, where you sat on the fireside seat
and we sucked on bitter chocolate covered toffees
squidging the rich, sweet centres.

Before that: milk-white ducks, with cornflake bills
flat out in breakfast bowls.

On heavy snow-logged days we flew on coalman's plastic sacks
filmed with a damp anthracite-face. School closed, ice-lagged pipes;
a drift as high as your head.

*Remember the knack of leaning right back
and taking your life in your hands?*

We watched the village from here. The clock tower hidden across the road
behind the private school's wood; its chimes marked our days and kept
our childhood nights awake.

Remember?

Armfuls of scrappy wood; hiding foiled potatoes.

A lifetime's dens hide from us.

Bird

Looks so smug
flicks up his tail feathers –
as if I care.

Do I?

Now he's gone.
The cat's appeared
like death on a warm day,

in two minds whether the effort
was worth a face full of feathers.

Other books published by Oversteps